Crows 2: Rings of Truth-The Afterthought

IHSAN JONES

Copyright © 2015 Ihsan Jones

All rights reserved.

ISBN:0998513105
ISBN-13:9780998513102

DEDICATION

This book is dedicated to my daughter and my sister, both of whom have had their private struggles. And to my granddaughter Kaya, who said not to "sugar coat", or "hold back" anything. "Tell your experience Grandma. The way it was and the way it happened."

As the burden bearer of truth in deliverance of a message, I will do exactly that! Make sure the message doesn't become" lost" inside the messenger.

CONTENTS

	Prologue	i
1	Soul Runner	Pg 5
2	Mind Channels:	Pg 12
	The Equation	
	The Clearness	
	The Opening	
	The Dreams	
	The Encounters	
	The Enlightenment	
3	Rings of Truth:	Pg 62
	Thoughts of a Clairvoyant	
	Bowels of the Ship	
	Epilogue	Pg 96

PROLOGUE

In life, everything must run its course. God gives us beliefs beyond measure. It is when we quantify it that we run into the problem. There is no equation that we can fixate ourselves on and be certain as to its outcome. God is the purpose, and life.

Understanding that the earth is built for containment of its inhabitants, as we explore, we get to see beyond what is measurable. Quantifying any derivative of its habitation can be exhausting and oftentimes leads to more discovery.

It is in the discovery that identifies the process. By no means can we have, see, taste and smell it all. It is our uniqueness that defines us. That separates us from other cohabitants. We are uniquely made to prosper and grow as a continuation.

We continue the cycle of completion until when and if there is an end. The end is not in sight but may be relevant towards the process.

I've met many creatures who've strangely identified me as being not of their world only occupied in it.

These creatures tell a tale that there is more, much more than we could ever fathom through our process of discovery.

They too, have a mission that they must complete. They cannot talk about their plans nor can we about ours. We're clueless as to what's the next step. Anyone that tells you otherwise is fooling themselves and you.

It's unique for us to have the ability to recognize greatness, power and influence. But in the eyes of what's to come, that greatness pales as meekness on this earth.

I submit, that as we go forward, one by one, we are not lost in the process. I truly believe that things will be shaken up in a way we know nothing about.

God is of purpose and for that reason has done everything on purpose, the purpose of which is the ultimate sacrifice for us to live and find out.

We will gather at our calling when the time comes. We will leave breathless and lifeless from what we've known. We won't look back as if we've left something because where we are going others are already waiting.

The end is not over when we are of purpose. It is a checkpoint to see how we have fared. Whether or not we're ready also is of no significance. It is the end of the tunnel or the terrain that we've tread. Buried on this earth, we will leave alive!

My book is about truths I have come to know. It is about an awakening of sorts.

"Yay, do I walk in the shadows of darkness, I fear no evil, nor shall man or woman fear what is complacent upon him/her"

It is the recesses of darkness that light has been shone. It is the mirror images as reminders of our faults and deeds. It is taking our place in the world as we know it not to run it or conquer it, but to live by its creed; that all man is created equal in the eyes of the Lord.

I tell my tale as it occurred, as things were inflicted upon me. And so it is with natural instinct that human emotion must run its course. You will see me from time to time battle with the saint (of my spirit) and the fear that must comply. We can never shelter ourselves or armor ourselves with shields that are strong enough to not be touched by mother- nature. Only when something has gone awry can we be this way. And since everything must take its place, in due course and due time, even that is common among us.

Everybody will not grow and mature. Everyone will not mature or ripen in the way the process seems that it should go. We all will succumb to our circumstances no matter what that is.

And it is with that, that I leave you to contemplate the, what if's and what is possible. More importantly, a doppelganger of hanging thoughts about The Unknown.

.

1 SOUL RUNNER

She would have to run and she knew it.

The car crept slowly as if the driver were reluctant to exceed the posted speed limit. Coasting along, she spied him with one eye all the while trying to maintain her composure. She decided to stare straight ahead as she sat next to him as if that would mask her plotting her escape. She was going to leave him and somehow he had known. Her heart was racing but she needed to remain calm to reassure him. He had control of her, complete control like he always did. He was her husband but the fears from the past couldn't erase the pain of not wanting to be with him. Once her feet hit the pavement he would be after her--he had planned to not let her go. She had to trick him, to win him over enough to convince him that she was on his side. She came to the realization that her fate could be dire if she was unreasonable in any capacity. She knew how he thought, sneaking a glance over her shoulder accidentally staring him directly in the face. Maybe he didn't notice. Perhaps he wouldn't think anything of it if she lowered her eyes or even cowered a little. She couldn't show strength, to him that would mean she thought she had the upper hand. He definitely had the upper hand. Prior to this, she had lost everything and in her mind, this would be their last ride together. If only she could convince him that she was being earnest. Only a fool would think twice about what she was doing. She needed to act quickly if her plan was to work. Her husband was a staunch man, full of dreams. He was smart, articulate and well respected. But it seemed that his life was ending when hers was only beginning. She had had relationships before but none like this; so controlling, so demanding of her time that she barely had any time for herself. It was all about him, their children, and this new domestic life that she thought she was prepared for but in reality, she just wasn't. It was sad that it had come to this. That she needed to get away for her freedom. Her sanity. There was no traffic and it was a lone street. Maybe cars parked on the side but that's what they do in residential neighborhoods. "Stop here," she said, "I'll be ready when you come back." She held back the tears and the fear that was thumping her heart. No time to think, feel, or have second thoughts about it. She hopped out. He kept his hand on the steering wheel without saying a word. She wasn't sure if he had bought it but he didn't protest to letting her out of the car. She glanced up the stairs. It was a steep climb. Once she arrived at the top of the porch she could see his car continue to drive slowly in the distance but she wasn't going to turn around. The door opened and she saw two young men standing guard. They were funny and making jokes. "My mama not home, one of them said. "We have to hurry. He might be back! I shouted.

"Nobody's coming in here. They'll have to get through us!"

The two guys were rough housing and acting tough. Throwing punches in the air, one of them was demonstrating what he would do if someone tried to come in. Flexing his arm muscles, they seemed hard as rocks and he was sure that no one could get past. Meanwhile, I was rushing through looking for my friend and a place to hide. I felt that it wasn't safe. On instinct, I grabbed the little girl that was standing in the middle of the floor and darted towards the couch. I crouched behind it with my arms covering her tightly. I looked for my friend but she wasn't home. I could sit still and be quiet but my body became restless. Angst with the thought of him rushing in, I took the little girl by the hand and moved to the kitchen. While there, I heard a loud noise. The door came swinging open as if had crashed from someone kicking it in. The element of surprise is what was on his side when he caught them off guard. I had forgotten to give them further warning of how big he was and how frightened I was of him. The two young men were like midgets in comparison yet and still they thought they were tough enough to take him on. Whoever he was, to them, they weren't afraid. The strong man stormed through the door and it was as if he had swept through everything that was in his path. Sucker punching one of them, he pounced on the other and managed to put them both in a headlock. With each one under his arm he smacked their heads together knocking them out. I ran as fast as I could with the little girl tucked neatly underneath my armpit running to safety. There was another flight of stairs right off the kitchen. I knew I had to reach them but there was only a small distance between me, him, and the stairs. My heels seemed to click as I headed towards them. A bright light was shining at the top leading the way. I leaped forward like a gazelle, my legs gliding gracefully over every other stair while holding steadily onto the little girl. He, on the other hand, was flying like a bat straight out of hell chasing after me. As I rose up the stairs, I could feel the man closely behind.

Then everything changed, momentarily drawing me closer towards the light.

The man never did catch up to me, but I knew somehow that the two young men, were not as fortunate.

I blinked, and felt that I was awake. During this strange twist of fate, I had now switched scenes:

There was no longer a little girl present, nor her friend's house, or the man whom she was familiar with, that was chasing her. But the young men were still in her dream. She could see them fighting in a large crowd. They were acting tough just as they did at the door when they tried to protect her. She grew weary and frantic as she watched the biggest one of the lot being in hot pursuit. He was looking for places to hide, to shake the man that was chasing him. He ran into a bathroom stall. The fight ensued. He broke free as others around him did and watched. He immediately looked for other places to run too. To escape. There were groups of people but no one stood out in the crowd. It was as if they didn't see him. He was alone. He saw a room and ran to it. There was a window. He could hear someone coming close bottling him in. He felt trapped. He wanted to yell outside of the window for the people standing in a group to help him. But he noticed they disappeared as he peeked his head out. Reluctant to leave the comforts of the building where he knew he might be safe, he looked both ways before climbing out. Over his shoulder there was commotion, he knew that someone was getting closer. He leaned one foot out the window hesitant to put it down. He felt vulnerable. Although there had been a massive crowd, no one it seems had been there for him. No one could see or hear him if he yelled. He found himself standing in the lone dark street with only bushes surrounding him. He could hide in a bush but there didn't seem to be enough cover. He could run, in any direction, but it was dark, lonely, and cold. He grew tired of the crowd that couldn't see, hear or protect him. This place had become lonely and cold when moments before he was acting tough with the rest of them. He stepped into the darkness undecided about his fate and disappeared into the night.

I struggled, thinking what did any of this have do with me? My mind had shifted or been altered to a scene that was taking place. I didn't know the participants but knew their characters. They portrayed people that I knew. A few days later someone dear to me, that I loved, had died. A bloodline connection and once again I had been given a sign. A sign that I could neither prevent nor alter. It had been destiny fulfilling its promise that the soul runner could not alter fate. That whatever was going to happen, there was no way of escaping it.

This was too much for me to handle. But it was not the end.

I had told my daughter the next day about the dream. She remained hopeful, like me that nothing would take place. Maybe nothing will happen? She said. We both prayed that it didn't but somehow deep inside, I knew otherwise.

I processed it different from her. She knew that whenever I told my dreams, there was always a ring of truth to it. And I knew that people's faces could be altered or shifted but that the similitude of what was happening would likely be carried out. I never knew, with my dreams who it could be or when or where. But I knew that the likelihood of them happening could overwhelm me. I stayed in panic mode and gave supplement and prayers. Maybe if I could sacrifice anything unworthy that I'd done for a chance to make it all go away. I'd give up being untruthful, if I had been, I'd give up mistreatment of anybody and everybody if that was the case. I knew I hadn't done anything wrong to my knowledge that deserved punishment but I was soul searching to find answers that could rectify the situation. If it was going to be me or one of my children, I wasn't capable of handling that. But also not capable of handling it for someone that I love. Someone that I was chained to by blood in bondage or marriage. This would be the most hurtful to me. That and explaining it while I was in angst. I couldn't eat or sleep while thinking about it and was a nervous wreck.

My soul is rectified with the truths my mind and heart embodies once the event is recognized.

CROWS 2: RINGS OF TRUTH-THE AFTERTHOUGHT

2 MIND CHANNELS

The Equation

Everyone wants to know what the Equation is. It is life and everything that's in it. It is death and all that's come to past. Here are snippets of what that life has taught me about the equation.

To begin with…

We're more complicated than what we create.

Our containment is for us to explore.

The Clearness is our guide. We can see and feel everything through it.

Understanding the Clearness will help us fundamentally understand ourselves.

We live to gather truths that expand our will. Those truths are defined by our living.

The guidance we receive is sort of offbeat yet driven.

It is offbeat because we can't yet make it out. It is driven because drive is what moves us.

We are biologically bound to the containment in which we live.

Our rhythm speaks volumes and our mass is sound.

We are co-creators of our own markers in life and thus co-conspirators in our destiny.

As we test our boundaries our brains and minds have stop gaps.

These stop gaps keep us from overloading.

When we overload our fragments are torn to pieces.

These pieces will continually try to become whole. It is their very nature to be together to work together with this rhythm-that is our function.

We continually try to seek happiness because happiness is our reward.

Our rewards are designed to heighten our passions. Our passions are designed to pro-create.

Promulgation of the species is to our advantage but we can be taken out one by one or in mass.

Living the Equation equips us yet for another.

The Equation is not of our choosing nor is remaining in it.

The Clearness

The clearness defines our purpose of who we are.

It is a live communication channel that is always on.

There is no downtime for the Clearness-even under the cloak of darkness it is clear.

Our night vision is like our minds, spectacular as we remember everything from the day yet it is cloaked and hidden so we stumble through it. We know not what we see yet we know that which is in the day remains.

We can see through the clearness. We drink, breathe, exist, survive and promulgate with what the clearness does.

The Clearness exists for us. And I am not talking about the atmosphere. I'm talking about the design as part of the Equation that separates worlds.

Worlds that live beyond us and can interact with us at any time.

How do I know this? Because I have seen it. I have seen the bridge of the divide of those reaching in. I have seen the promulgation of thoughts that suggest entities unknown.

I have seen those beside us that alternate in another realm and collect or connect with our thoughts.

I have witnessed their precious bodies, their words, expressions, their concerns.

Life as we know it is not all that there is.

There are some of us who will intertwine with revelation.

What's revealed now are glimpses.

The glimpses come from Guides. Our Guides are attached to our markers.

We are given suggestions both implanted and blatantly.

We are constantly being readied for our departure.

Any intervention is timed and planned but can be altered or delayed at the will of our makers.

The brain is shielded because it is important. Our tiny eyes are windows. Our window panes are clear. We must be able to see through the souls of others otherwise our interactions are fruitless.

Our bodies are reflected like shadows.

These shadows represent the duplex of our nature.

Our shadows show us that we are always here, that someone is watching and that we can't run away.

The clearness is our makeup. Everything must be clear in order to see through it.

The clearness is said to be absence of color where everything shows up.

Nothing can exist without the clearness. The air we breathe, the water we drink, the mirrors we fashion out of rock (mass) to reflect.

The shiny objects are there to remind us of who we are. So we can see ourselves and know that we are important.

We could never see ourselves without the clearness.

The clearness is meant to be spacious so that our containment seems infinite.

Everything can only go so far before it breaks up into the atmosphere and dissipates-even traveling at light speed has its limits.

The stratosphere is an ominous illusion reaching so high above as to represent limitless.

The disconnected off beat and disjointed messages we are sent sometimes are time pieces of our past and future.

We don't have the capacity to put it all together because it wasn't designed for us to do so.

Our intellect is fearless and knows no bounds. Our tenacity is ferocious and yet tamed. Our ability to tend to our affairs on a daily basis is indicative of who and what we are and how we're feeling.

If it were up to us we'd ask the questions when our mental capacity allows us to do so.

If it were up to us we would be given the answers to those questions immediately and with resolve.

Each creature that is created has a Maker. Those makers although different-promulgate (collaborate).

The earth is part of something bigger. We are constantly trying to explore.

The world of amazement is never diminishing.

In our minds we have barely touched the surface.

Each generation must come into their own.

We live for comforts.

Our thinking minds become exhausted.

Our weary bodies must regenerate and be refueled.

The food that we eat dies as we eat it.

Something must die in order for us to live.

Nothing gets wasted. Everything is used.

The earth is like a sponge.

Everything must hold its order and stay in its place.

The animals have a different calling. They do their part in their own way.

We do not have to understand everything that exists nor does it have to understand us.

The human mind is complicated. You cannot see what the mind fully contains.

Without the body the mind will not exist.

Our lights can be dampened and our minds will still function but in a reduced capacity.

We may never realize our true achievement.

The mind is a never ending wasteland, brilliant yet subtle.

Thoughts are processed at will but sometimes thoughts are planted.

Mediums interact on our behalf at all times. Those mediums are by things we may not understand.

Mediums exist as guide posts and checkpoints.

Those checkpoints are for our protection.

If we were shown something it is because we are supposed to see it.

Regardless of how we live, our exit must be the same. Funneled through a channel of optimism and exchange.

Once there-we have reached our capacity.

All lights will turn on and be the brightest we have ever seen. The walls leading our path is Blank.

Things to know about the Clearness:

Water is cleansing

Air is refreshing

Reflection is power

Shadows are necessary

Illumination is transitional

Transmission is imminent

Disintegration is inevitable

Promulgation is essential

Blankness is the Beginning and End.

The puzzle has been solved in the Containment and it is that Life exists in a Bubble.

The Equation is much larger than this not necessarily in size but in Capacity.

Minuteness doesn't mean diminished and death isn't finite.

Flying doesn't mean higher and swimming far below doesn't mean you've sunk.

Simultaneous is a word that Must be Used.

Before and After Define- The End.

 There is no such thing as a loss. Everything is always found by something or someone and is always useful.

One thing can't exist without the other when it comes to death and regeneration.

Now let's tackle some of the Biggest Questions…

Life begets life and our Makers are not Ourselves. We are born with the capacity to Live. Death is a necessary component for each and every living thing. Death does not mean the end-it is an appropriation for existence.

Existence and transition are not opposite of each other they are simultaneous. Our world though we may not understand it is readying us for something else.

When the channels of communication are bent, the walls are broken down (thus the barriers).

We do not empty our chairs when we empty our spirits-we leave markers along the way.

So What about…

The doctrines that we expose to ourselves…

They Are For The Comforts Of Man.

Because life cannot be received is such a way to make us full – we must grasp for, construct and exist in every comfort known to man including that which we fabricate in our minds thus giving us reason to ease our pain and enjoy the bliss.

There's a reason that we think. It is to stretch our capacity. But what we know has been dormant all the time. We release it in increments as we become smarter by our exposure. The process of deduction and elimination (reasoning) enriches us yet leaves us reduced. We reduce our power as we live on. We expend our energy at our highest peak.

Our energy is not meant to drain but to be passed through the channels. It revives with time and continues on to be useful.

We cannot distinguish the Power That Is. We must go through our process knowing that we are limited. But if we strive all we can in every way possible, we've succeeded.

Success is not tangible, rewards are.

Having an open mind is important to dialogue. The mind's eye sees plenty when our breath of knowledge expands.

An open mind means an open doorway but even if the lungs are filled to capacity, when the air is stagnant, it will still fill the room thus closing off the ability to take in any more air. Religion is like air. It will fill you up but can become stagnant with its hidden principles.

The Clearness is All Things Possible, not only life sustaining but also our Guide.

Living in a funnel or as wide and spacious, it is our souls that Clearly let us see.

When we ascertain our truth- it is what we will bear witness too. We limit our capacity, when we douse our spirit, we turn down the lamps on our lights. We also take baby steps towards fulfillment. It is necessary so as not to overload.

Man does not have the wherewithal to see and hear everything. What we know is not all that we know. But what we know is who we are. Dormant lies the spirit of the man seeking to be free. The boundaries we set for ourselves were not meant to be confining. We explore capacities unknown. We assimilate with like kind and like species. Crossing over boundaries is not allowed. Your capacity for fullness comes from within. When we seek knowledge we seek fullness.

Fullness is a form of satisfaction. Satisfaction is what keeps us going regardless of the way it is attained.

Our scope is limited by our vision. Our lens is constantly being readjusted and focused. Focus is what the real world is all about. Focusing on what is necessary to keep you alive.

Our books of knowledge can all burn tomorrow and we will still live. It is from within ourselves that all knowledge is bound.

If the Entities want, they can take us at any time. It is their duty to do so.

An Entity is what has been revealed to us. Everyone has seen, heard or interacted with and Entity.

We don't have a name for what we can't process.

Therefor the process must be pure. Pure is what we can't see, everything else we can and pure is as Clear as it gets.

The Opening

I think that we leave blank, discarding any doctrines or philosophies. They were there for our comforts, conveniences, confessions and civilities.

But our capacity for healing was always there. Our prayer spoke to God regardless of what cloth or headgear we were wearing.

Gods' eyes meet's ours through the lens peering deep down into our souls. When our eyes tear, we weep. God hears and there is intervention. It is a process that repeats itself over and over. The internal fortitude that we have comes from the strength that God gives. God lends a hand at the right time and on time.

When we're fragmented we must piece together continually seeking to become whole. It is the piecing together that is the healing process. Like puzzle pieces finding its place. And when it doesn't, there's compensation.

Religion is compensation. A formality that we perform to help us feel that we are getting it right. Rituals that are established as easement and appeasement. But religion isn't the tell all of our story. Religion is the actions that we must carry out. Our deeds are fortified by faith and that is bigger than any religion. Our actions outwardly reflect our cultures and norms. But the piecing together and the healing is a continual struggle. We are what we know and what we demonstrate (at the time) but like the earth-we are also a sponge taking in all that surround us in this containment and that's why we know there can be so much more. The ultimate healing is to know all the answers, that which we are not given. Piecing it together and our own way broadens our capacity but makes us fall short from the mark but it is innately within us to do so.

The mediums are there as guideposts because God does not speak to us directly. Many have longed for a conversation with God but it is as riddles and puzzles. We are built into the equation and protected. Our worlds are separate for a reason. Reasons that we aren't supposed to know for now. Speculative and truncated whims that take us on tangents are not the answer. It is The Opening that will reveal itself in due time. Where others reside that will invite us there. Taking us not at our convenience but when they feel we are ready. We will be taken out of the equation and brought into another realm of existence. Leaving our bodies, our thoughts and our minds behind. They will be our markers holding our place. Acting as placeholders for others to learn from. I have heard it and seen it and know it's there. It exists simultaneous as we breathe and eat. The more we know and seek to know, the closer we are to it. But it is the Opening that must arrive, that takes us there.

Its inhabitants are waiting. If you ask enough questions you may be given the answers. It may not be a convenient time or expedient. But it will be the right time because it will be your time to go. And death is imminent (a precursor), for getting there.

You will leave your body behind as you walk the path. The path that has been lit and bright. The blank wall will serve as your guide ridding you of all defense. You won't need it in the place you are going. All answers will be given and all eyes will be placed on you as you are taken there.

8888888888888

This is what I saw, what I felt and what I heard.

The astonishment of the act not being carried out is what woke me up. The taking back of the hand (swiftly moving), but it was still in time enough to see the Others as I am sure it was meant to be. I was given a glimpse of what's to come.

The Dreams

I thought the dreams would stop. But they didn't. I was hoping there would be a long time in between them. But it wasn't. My dreams had intensified and somehow I knew that ending them (like I stated before) would be the end of me. My dreams can't end until I end, and that's a fact. Even if my progeny continues them, it will be as an extension and likely their own.

I thought that ending the first book 'When Crows call' could end my pain, end my nightmares. But closing a chapter in one book was like opening another. The dreams weren't going to stop until they were done with me being a medium. A medium to disseminate them. The never ending story that I saw myself caught up in was the recurring cycles and patterns (of dreams). By now they had spun out of control because of their intensity. Intensity is what I had felt on the freeway when I was driving along…

It was a clear bright morning and I was doing my usual, taking the grandbabies to school. The stretch of the freeway to get there wasn't too long-a few miles. I entered the freeway merging into the slow-paced traffic. It was normally this way but today was moving kind of steadily. I was on autopilot for driving because I knew the route well.

I'd zigzag from one lane to another depending on which was going the fastest. After I'd reach the overpass I knew I was home free. It was side roads from there on the rest of the way. I drove past the water each day on the side facing the shore. It was pleasant to see the waves bouncing off the suns reflection at sunrise. The crystal clear water was a stark contrast to the hustle and bustle of the freeway. I had made it down now all I had to do was make it back up. The kids were let out the car. I could do this with my engine running as they were big enough to run inside. I pounced up ahead and turned the corner wiggling my way through the streets to get back on the freeway. Going back was always easier I could drive a lot faster. Without traffic standing in my way I was up to normal speed around 65 to 70 mph. I could hurry to get home if I wanted or I could stop off to get coffee. My habit was to go either way depending on which took precedent.

My mind was drifting into a fog. I had already thought about it on the way down but going back was worse. I was in deep thought. Too deep to be driving at the time only I didn't know.

I had made it safely to drop them off but I kept thinking about the dreams, the deaths, and the encounters. It was a closed chapter in my life I thought that had been resolved. The pain was still lingering. I hurt from knowing so many loved ones had died and wanted to know why. Why now? Why so soon? Why so suddenly?! The ogre had kept its promise and told me about it. Something I said I would never do, once I close the book.

It was like a whirlwind in my head spinning uncontrollably. I didn't even know I was thinking that deep until I was in it and that's when everything else became secondary. I'd forgotten where I was for a moment until the sound of the loud horn reminded me. The big rig had shaken me. I was awakened and startled at the same time.

How could I be in such a trance like state on the road? And so much so that it could have killed me.

I swerved instantaneous barely missing the divide.

The divide was up high separating the overpass. The same overpass I'd taken to get there but in the opposite direction on the way back. There was no riding down the water on the way back. I wanted to get home quickly in case I still needed some sleep. But my car was moving in the direction of the route I'd taken to get coffee and I didn't know why. I knew I didn't have time to make that kind of run that morning. My daughter had already called me in the night before telling me I needed to babysit. I was supposed to go to her house and pick up her child. As I remembered this the last few seconds coming out of my fog (trance) after the big rigs horn, I had attempted to revert to the right and go underneath. All lanes were full of cars driving fast. How I thought I could do this, I don't know. My reaction to turn the wheel kept me going straight. I had avoided a horrific accident. One that could have been fatal.

Then a thought came to mind, *"death can sometimes keep quiet and still, but it can also be violent and horrific!"*

I had gotten my answer. Contemplating death, and the horrible ways in which it can occur, had me imagining the worse.

The intimate conversation I'd had with the ogre was understood. That just because you're questioning the process, doesn't mean that you would be spared from its wrath.

"You won't believe what just happened?" I told my daughter talking on my cell phone as I was exiting the freeway. I had her on speakerphone but still needed to pull over. I parked at the first spot I could.

I tried to explain to her the magnitude of my almost crashing. I told her how fast I was going and how high up I was. I explained that if the big rig hadn't honked its horn I could have possibly flew up on the freeway after hitting the divide and ending up below, not to mention the other catastrophes and casualties that could have resulted from this such as the big rig smashing into me and making it worse.

"Mom! Stop it! She yelled. Can't you see what you're doing? You're attracting this to you! Don't you remember? The law of attraction-the secret, remember?"

I thought about it for a moment. Oh yes, I do remember watching the DVD about that a few years ago. But what did that have to do with it? Maybe she did have a point.

I continued driving thinking maybe there was something to what my daughter had said. But when I got home I switched gears. I knew I wasn't attracting this to myself, couldn't be. I had no reason to be thinking about death except for the recent events that were still weighing heavy on my mind and I was still grieving about. But it wasn't death that stayed on my mind. And it wasn't my choice to be in such deep thought about it on the freeway. I didn't know this chain of events would happen. That I would have to barely miss death to be given a message. A profound message that was on a broader scale. To say that it's not the why or how (that death occurs) but that it's not personal.

It doesn't matter if you die in your sleep or die in a horrific manner, death is still death and it's something that you can't avert when it's your time to go.

My resolve with this wasn't over. But at the time I'd hoped it would be.

THE ENCOUNTERS

The encounters were such that they needed more explaining. In my first book I'd written about them as they occurred. In this book I have tied them together and put them in perspective. If the encounters were a teaching tool, then it is a lesson that I am still learning.

All I can tell you is what I saw, and the way it happened.

The first encounter was when I was a little girl. It was my first interaction with what I consider to be the unknown or paranormal. And it wasn't something that actually happened to me but what I observed.

I couldn't have been more than 8 to 10 years old because my nephew was still a baby. Well a toddler because he could talk and walk. My mother was babysitting him. In the middle of the night I was awakened by crying and screaming. He swung his hands wildly stomping on the floor. My mother was trying to hold him to restrain. This continued on for about a minute. She quieted him down he will continue to "they're going to get me!" Every now and then he breaks loose in general then she tried to start all over again holding them down. "What's going to get you?" My mother asked. The spiders! My nephew was pointing to the floor as if he was surrounded and needed to flee. My mother, being the kindhearted person that she is, consoled him and rocked him there no spiders you say and if there are all get them! She pretended to stamp them out.

I stayed awake long after my nephew had fallen asleep but not without being in her arms.

"Mama, I asked. What was that?" It was the devil riding his back she would say. That was her way of explaining a nightmare.

This struck me as a child and each time I'd go to sleep I say a prayer so that the devil-wouldn't ride my back.

"Now I lay me down to sleep, I pray the Lord my soul to keep, and if I die before I wake, I pray the Lord my soul to take."

When the Ogre presented itself it was under the cover of darkness. It lurked in the shadow and almost stayed back. I'd seen its shape and form (the part that wasn't hidden anyway) and the slight beam of light that revealed it was subtle. It was here all along, like everything else. It was capable of appearing as did The Others when I encountered the Opening. But I didn't get the impression that the Ogre as it called itself was evil. "I am the ogre of death", it said. I come when it is time to take you out of the equation" (not me literally), but as in that *was* its job. It did not come at that time for any other purpose but to be known. I was to be introduced to what the Ogre is. What that force is that beckons us as God(s) call. It is a dutiful attendant bearing emotion almost as if talking to Dr. Spock, its pure logic on display for what it was saying to make sense. It is not swayed one way or the other by what it does. It is doing a job. Which implies that it answers to someone or something. What I did see was mind blowing because who could have thought that something so devastating to humans could look so humble or nimble. Something that strange that appeared before me was talking and communicating. I wasn't afraid, but more or less stunned as the conversation progressed. A shocker from what I would hear plain as day. The message was intended for me and came from a small tan lump of mass possibly gooey in substance with a funneled head that shaped like a flat top cone. I couldn't have be the more- wiser, for it. And I will never forget what the lady (the nurse) said at the hospital as I make the correlation. "They cannot help you. No one can."

It was a warning. A warning that what you are about to see or witness in your forth coming days only you will be privy to. And that whether or not you choose to disseminate (share) it, no one will believe you.

That's why I say they are safe. Safe from us ever knowing (in the world) unless it is shown.

No nurse was capable of being that evil on her own. To have been acting so strange for no reason. But there was a reason and a purpose to her strangely occupied madness. It was to prepare me for my meeting with The Ogre (and the other entities). I wasn't clear on why she had done this and I knew there could be bad seeds in every profession. I was befuddled, dazed and confused, scratching my head at a loss.

I figured it was out of pure meanness and that the lady was the kook that she was trying to say that the doctor was. But it wasn't. It was a startling revelation of what was to come. I had been prepped so to speak, that odd things, strange things might happen as a result of my query. My query on asking, why and how to God. It had come at a much later date and at a cost. A cost of me questioning my sanity. It was easy to tell people about the nurse because she was tangible in the flesh and tales of mistreatments in hospitals are actually not that uncommon. But the way she did what she did and the why is now known to me.

I'm not even aware if she knows it in retrospect. I have never gone back to visit that hospital again let alone have seen this nurse. I wonder as with the nursing home, if she really was a part of their staff or there only for me or if her soul was taken over or was she there serving time, acting out her penance to this life in some way. I have so many questions about the nurse. Ones that I Really, probably *don't* want to know the answers to.

But what does resonate with me besides her actions is what she said.

"They cannot help you. No one can.

They won't believe you.

I have the power to make the doctor do whatever I say.

Whatever orders I write with this pen, the doctor will follow.

I have the power to send you home or to the nursing home."

She was having a conversation with herself. All I could do was be mesmerized and listen. Whether or not I went home meant everything as far as my care. The nursing home would be a more professional place. So I thought. But it was at this point that I was preferring home in spite of not being able to walk or have someone capable of caring for my injuries.

I preferred home, to death in these places, which is what I thought would happen given all the strange circumstances.

But I had survived. And it was for a reason. I wasn't to have chance encounters as in the hospital and nursing home, I was to have purposeful meaning.

I believe they are safe. Safe from ever being known unless it is supposed to happen.

The entities are safe because they can lurk in the shadows appearing in broad daylight or be subdued in their renderings with you by being cloaked in the atmosphere swirling like thickened wind.

I understand what the kook means as far as what the lady (the nurse) implies. It meant that I would be unbelievable to everybody when revealing what I saw and that I would be deemed a kook for doing so.

That is the risk that I have to take.

Her calling a competent man such as a doctor something as outlandish as a kook is a bit extreme unless she has personal knowledge and when she first stormed into my hospital room she implied that she didn't! "Who was that?!" She asked emphatically.

She then became possessed and acted out accordingly. He's a kook! She announced. I've seen him walking around here with his head up in the clouds spaced out. He can't help you! She then followed up with the words…No one can, unless I say so.

It was the strangest thing that had ever happened to me, from a human standpoint and I was rendered helpless in explaining it.

I told my daughters about the nurse who they became disgusted. They wanted to storm the hospital to have a meeting with her and perhaps beat her up. "Mom, you could have at least reported her!" One of my daughters said to me having had no satisfaction of revenge. "I did", I said. Quietly knowing that that wouldn't have made a difference anyway.

I was to be the Kook that she referenced. A very competent lady with degrees and credibility reduced to rubbish by her words. The world would be watching and waiting to hear my story and she knew I was the One to tell it. Her chiding came as a warning to myself and others that telling about the entities that exist alongside God in Gods Kingdom will render you a Kook!

It's that plain and simple. I had to think about it. To tell or not to tell.

With every key stroke I pecked as if my last. My hush, hush demeanor wasn't for naught. I had to quietly conquer my fears of thinking that as I lay the words on the paper (with my pen) my story would not make it out there in the universe where it is meant to be told.

Everything was at stake. My reputation, my children's welfare, my well-being, even my sanity.

I had to question whether or not I was doing the right thing. If the timing was right for people to know about what exists, what else is out there besides, us.

But just like the dreams, as they come to me. I had to tell them. But at first, only to trusted souls (my children).

Everything was coming to me at a whirlwind. It was happening so fast. I had had more encounters in this past year than I had had in my entire life. I had questioned it. I didn't understand why. Was it because I was asking? Or was it because the chain of events that were inevitable to play out I was to be privy to. And my savvy wit no matter how distraught would have to bear witness.

I felt like an intelligent fool being played with. A pawn in a sea of exchange and interaction.

I had no remedy for what I was experiencing except to tell it. Was I bold enough? Would it be believed?

It didn't matter.

That death is final is the reason we're here. That life is never eternal in the form in which we think it is another.

I find myself watching the stars (the signs), not literally but figuratively for something that abates me. Something that says God favors you and that's why you were chosen.

Otherwise, what else is it for? Why should I have a need to know?

Chosen to have talks with the Ogre. Chosen to see things in time and space before they happen. Chosen to be shown a hand by God and to be touched and spared in the process.

And what does chosen mean, for lack of a better word?

Does it mean to be anointed because you are disseminating information that only few others have come across or does it mean that you are thrust in a game of wait and see and only time will tell its outcome.

I now that I must die. I am not afraid of that anymore.

Although I do close closets as I walk by them for fear of striking up a conversation with the Ogre.

I should battle my fears, conquer them. But it is not up to me. God has given us the full gamut of emotions to be dealt with. We can't run away and hide from them. Nor can we wish them away. Our emotions are who we are, good or bad.

If I shall be deemed a kook, so be it but the truth shall set you free. (In my mind anyway).

****

So Is There Evil in the World?

I had a 'breach of consciousness', it was a spirit awakening.

A moment where I had reconciled truths with many falsities I'd held. I was so busy living in the "conjuring" that the thought of what's "really" happening hadn't crossed my mind. I had to live with what I saw and that's a fact.

We all do. We conjure up spirits with rituals that have been passed as hand me downs when in fact they are mostly only near the truth. The fact that God made us is what we know. How we define God or Gods is what has been up for debate. We don't always see God as something that controls everything when in fact that is the truth.

I was as an administer of justice at times as all beings are and thus hold the attributes of the Ogre-as we all do. We have the capability of halting time, interrupting and ending life just like the ogre. In most cases this is done without remorse and pre-thought. Thus at times, when it comes to other creatures we are capable of reacting without vengeance and have common bonds and have become mediums by which to administer justice. We can act without conscious on ending that creature's life simply by stepping on it. We may even be unawares. But at the very moment our paths cross, a decision is made.

"Vengeance is mine said the Lord" (a quotation from perhaps, biblical scripture) thus we are incapable of escaping judgment.

But that judgment must come full circle and in due time because the wrath has already been set.

All life is a perceived threat and can be killed. If we act on it, act to kill, to harm with malice and deceit, this is the evil in the world. . .

It is our job to sacrifice life to sustain ourselves where most of it occurs as naturally and without pre-thought or malice. We are halting and interrupting a life as we know it in order to sustain ourselves.

A planned or random attack like animals do, is no different from ours. A just and more human way of eating them is what we have.

But evil is different. Evil is lack of compassion or remorse for what preceded you in death. Carrying out the act as a horrendous deed. These deeds are punishable and will find their way back around to us in some way or fashion even if we are unawares. Insidious delusional acts are a crime too even if the person is incapable of ascertaining it. Our thoughts can persuade us to cross the border with no check points in place and this is truly evil.

God is watching at all times. God knows your capabilities beforehand. So what's important to know about evil is that it must be keep in check. Every opposite has its desired effects. Good and bad are a clear choice though we may be caught up in the moment. We are guilty as charged when we commit these sins. Unfortunately, the definition of evil is within our capacity to do so.

But it is different from what the Ogre does. The Ogre, it says, is doing its job. What it's supposed to do. Therefor the Ogre is incapable of discerning the degree of heinousness with which it takes you out (of the equation). You must go-when it's your time to go- and that's all it knows-that's what it must do.

I get the impression that the ogre is summoned on someone else's behalf. That God is in it somehow someway. And to say that is cruel, although death in our eyes is, that would be to say that God(s) are (cruel). But God(s) creates balance.

As others go-more will be brought forth. The life and death cycle is part of the equation.

The Swirlies presented another dilemma. I did feel threatened. But I am not to live in fear because that's not what I believe was intended. It was a message.

I couldn't run or hide or ignore them. The voices speaking through the wind loud and clear. In a high pitch overtone as if relay signals trying to come though. Maybe I wasn't supposed to hear it. But I did. So what am I to make of it? It can only be Gods watchers, keepers intervening in a way that they possibly could. I can only say that I am glad that they didn't do what they said they should do. "We should just kill her! it said, while one was listening to the other. It was a conversation amongst themselves that I overheard.

How could I possibly tell someone this and make them believe me? Something like that could make you go crazy out of fear of watching, waiting to see if they will come back. But I try not to think about it because I am a strong believer. I know that it wasn't meant to be or God would have allowed it. But was this borderline evil, I didn't know. It was said with malice and there was ill intent. And although the ogre is neutral in its authority with what it is charged with, the swirlies presented a different story- something else. They defied time, space and altered the atmosphere with their renderings of sound and movement. I could hear them plain as day, but I couldn't see them. Only the clearness being swirled right in front of me. I can't really say what their purpose was either. They didn't talk to me like the Ogre. They only spun in circles stirring up the atmosphere. The contrast of the ogre and swirling beings is a dilemma. The ogre stayed in the shadows and partially hid itself. Only its great mass and color showing thick in texture yet solid in substance. A small tan creature only so tall and was mid- air and not on the ground. Exposing it as such clears my consciousness and thus I feel free.

Does that help me understand death better? Perhaps. Do I know that life must end? Yes I do. Do I believe that we go someplace else (besides earth)? Yes I believe that we are taken there. So our souls are not lost, and after death there's a new beginning or a continuation of our passing leading through the passageway.

The ancients have studied this. It's spoken of in scripture. I have always believed because the world is bigger than us and there is too much to know. But my faith has increased tenfold because of the encounters. To me that was tangible proof that something else exists.

I can only be humbled by my experience not more scared. I must look at the world and everything in it as God's creatures capable of doing well, just about almost anything.

And there is no conjuring of any creature we can do scarier than what we've already seen. There is practically every combination of plant and animal known to man so making hybrids is unnecessary. That is man playing with the gifts he/she has been given. The monsters we draw are already something that possibly exists in a non- threatening form unless we cross its path and are considered food or a threat to its survival. I don't believe in demons. I believe in other creatures created by God for their own purpose exclusive of ours. There are many creatures we may never know about or even see, new ones are being discovered every day.

So evil, is not God. And the devil does not ride your back.

But what happens is a captivation of spirit altering your attention drawn upon by the references you know to make it easier and more palatable but also it is what God wants you to know.

Can we explain this to children? Some prefer the simple concept of God versus the devil. The devil being Gods adversary. It's simple and easier to digest on a young brain. But should we be instilling fear instead of love and reverence? Surely we must teach our own the way we see fit, but I believe there is so much more than we could ever know.

Especially since I have been chosen to see and experience the Others first hand. I cannot lie to a child but I may simply opt out of explaining it. They should not be thinking about death when it is time for them to live. They too will find the answers in their own time when they are mature enough and ripe enough to digest it. Gods path is for everyone regardless of which of them we choose to take.

****

The dreams are figurative and symbolic.

That events played out similar to my dreams, may seem unreal, but isn't. The brain shuffles through real life experiences altering your conscious. So how do I get a handle on what's real and what isn't? What's tangible, I can see, touch and feel, also what's not? The medium that you have thus becomes a reference point. In my case the crows, and dreams. This is my greatest dilemma to date. How to rectify the seen with the unseen. This has been my greatest quandry to date. The crows are tangible and real they seek me out. The dreams, they happen to me in my sleep, or at least start out that way. I suppose they call it a higher calling when your spirit receives the signals that no longer are blocked coming through some way, somehow, loud and clear. God is of purpose and in a purposeful way will give us a message. It speaks to our capacity, knowing that we can receive the signals that come through regardless of how discerning they may seem. Knowing what's to come has always been a shocker to me. I am always surprised yet not surprised if there is such a thing. A natural phenomena occurring about life and death or illness mostly upsets me because it is unknown upon whom it will occur.

My life is sorted out in phases. There is the phase of knowing what I saw and walking amongst them. And the phase of having seen, heard and been exposed to things. How do you rectify the spirit having participated in this and still take care of the mundane (everyday tasks that we must abide by in your everyday living?). In some way my capacity is increased. But God is not complacent nor can I be. I should be resounding with joy of the natural calling that I have-the knowledge that our makers exist. They come to me with as natural spirit inanimate in the world for reasons unknown to man, telling me stories as I go along adjusting the rhythms with their latitude. Altering space and time if only for a mere second to tell me that God is made of miracles to mankind and that life exists and we shall be set free. The Containment as part of the equation is part of destiny fulfilled.

****

Of the last two dreams I had one of them almost frightened me out of my skin. They came within days of each other. One was considered to be somewhat pleasant (in the end anyway) and it took me walking the marina the next day to get its full meaning. I'm going on faith as I think about it because as we speak I still have shockers running through body. The fact that it came so close and hit close to home makes my spine tingle and I sometimes get shudders just thinking about it. Here is the first dream:

Dream # 8

"There was a living room with people standing around. They were about to pull up chairs. A faint voice could be heard in the background saying that it was alive. No one could hear that voice. The living room was set up as if a funeral would take place. The person's body had vessels dangling from it. Something kept asking, "How could you live without the body?" The voice kept repeatedly saying, "I'm alive". Then the scene switched to the kitchen. Passing through the kitchen were voices that could help. One lady in particular was sought out. The lady instead, stopped to get her hair and nails done. Then she danced and sang on the beach as if there were no care or worries in the world. She began to swing her hair freely along with the wind as if nothing else mattered. The person with the faint voice lifted their head. The dream ended."

Immediately after the dream I felt compelled to tell it. Through my shakes and quivers I texted my two daughters. I would have texted all of them but all of them weren't accessible. I was reluctant the most to tell my oldest daughter, her best friend had recently died and was part of the cycle after taking to the Ogre.

I had no idea she would come back and be in my dream. To me it was to send a message to my daughter that she was ok. That was what I got out of it but also something else. It was also why I spared my daughters ears of the graphic details telling her only the pleasant parts. I didn't spare this on my other daughter however, I told her the entire dream feeling that she had no direct connection to it. "I think she; Rya wants you to know she's Ok. When I saw her she was swinging her braids like a child as if she was free, with no worries. That was the message I was supposed to give. I walked the marina the next morning feeling good about my interpretation of what the dream meant, so much so that I write about it on Facebook. The social media had become my outlet but for me my connection on fb was to family and friends. I wanted to share the joy that I felt while walking along the shore bright and early.

But in the recesses of my mind I knew there was something else. Something that had to do with the graphic nature of the gory details of that dream. Something I tried to suppress until arriving at my car after that pleasant walk. The parking lot was empty except for maybe about three cars. There was one sitting next to mine and at the opposite end of the parking lot. What struck me first as I approached, was how many.

I started counting with each step I took. By the time I got to 16 I thought I was done but then I looked up and counted another, 17 crows were lined up overhead and around my car. I approached softly not to startle them. There was one that was pecking beside me hopping along as if to greet me as I emerged from the trees, walking along as if to make sure id notice.

I'd been to this park many times before and there were never any birds-crows. But on this day they stood out.

How could I have met the birds after having such pleasant thoughts? It was meant to be.

Two days later my daughter called me with the news. She had gone to the emergency room with what she apparently had thought was a cold or flu, perhaps even pneumonia. She was checked out and screened for what it could be. She left the emergency room on her way home. She then received a call that shook her and caused her to go back. We've found a mass, the doctors said. And just for precaution we'd like you to come back and take an x-ray. My daughter did. But it was not good news. My real worries had just begun.

She explained to me that the mass they found could be cancer and that she wouldn't know until she takes follow up tests.

I went home and cried.

How could her news have been so immediate and right after my dream?

Then I had another.

The second dream however was much worse than the first. So much so that I had begun screaming in the middle of the night loud enough to possibly wake my neighbors.

THE CLEARNESS cont.

In the Clearness nothing is hidden. Even if it is covered or locked inside (of something) it is still present. The clearness contains everything. The shadows reveal it someway somehow as it shows up as mass. A silhouette of some sort contains its shape. Everything that's synergistic to the earth is contained here. The saying, 'you can run but you can't hide-has meaning. It's saying that no matter where you go you are capable of being found-or showing up. Therefore, the clearness is our guide as well as our veil (like a shade) that separates us from those that control or have dominion over the containment. God or Gods- they are our makers and know everything about the containment (our living quarters) a part of, (the Equation).

The Clearness is that which channels our fullness yet breaks it into pieces.

It keeps us together until it is time to dissipate. Its dual force has properties that bend with time and as it opens up, we can see our directors, orchestrators, in another realm.

The clearness just happens: we don't ask for it. We are thrust into it in human form along with the many other species we may or may not know. Each species has a definable path. It's likely chosen already.

Each must choose which way it will live and how it will survive. Some of it is predesigned as arranged among the choices. We must coexist with these beasts and animals knowing that God has full knowledge of how we exist. Their world is separate from ours but homogenous with like kind. Our kindred spirits meet at twilight as we rest to replenish and fulfill ourselves. We are passerby's like strangers in a car riding different waves but traveling in the same direction. We never link the blood except as food. What we consume from one another merges us as one. These are our only possibilities otherwise we must remain separate as it was intended to be.

We are bound by our confinement. And though it may appear to be spacious we are rebounded by the pressure in which our bodies can stand. We can only go so far up as well as down even if a tool is used such as a spacecraft. It won't be long before we can break the barriers that hold us down but the unseen barriers are part of the Clearness. Everything is right before our eyes like an illusion or a mirage. It is there, but time takes it away reshaping it back to its original form only to be used again by another generation. Spacious and wide our breath appears to occupy what appears to be nothing. Our lens (eyes) are controllable in the clearness and show up as clear themselves. They mirror back to us what is reflected. If I look into a pair of eyes I can see myself, it also takes a clear lens (glasses) to correct vision that is corrupted.

If we look for anything to define us it should be the Clearness. The clearness is right before our eyes therefor we see yet we do not see. What better way to cloak the realm than that? I think it is ingenious!

The night shade which is pulled down still holds everything that was in the daylight. It doesn't move change shapes or shift forms. It is the nocturnal creatures emerging from the pattern they've been built for.

The Equation is like a live wire that's never turned off. A cycle of interchange and exchange that is dynamic working in form. We are clearly definable by nature with our distinctive roles and patterns. The nocturnal side is no different from the day, they must eat to survive just like we do. The pattern is already chosen for us that we must be a part of the life and death process. Don't look past the Clearness if you want to see God. Wait until it opens up and you are taken there. Our lens reveals many things but our lens does not reveal God. The clearness is a barrier that is aligned with infinity. We cannot alter or remove the clearness. Infinity to us is knowing that the earth has not yet been consumed. We will live on forever we hope even if it's through our progeny morphing ourselves into different versions. All is not lost if there is no heaven or hell. We are still here as long as God allows us to be. Our markers are left in our place and our spirit never dies. We are unburdened with having to remember who we were once before that's why we live on in a child-like spirit as if renewed. I can't tell you how many times I've seen someone (through the face of their child) look as though they've come back.

But it is not us. Not really, not anymore. It is a part of us. A significant part of us. It is our bloodline that will continue through the ages.

In order to live something else must die. Whether it is in plant or animal form it was living. Therefor life sustains itself by rejuvenating through death and the clearness is our passageway as well as our containment. We will be consumed by the earth but our shadows show us that our spirits will live on. We will always reflect the shadows of life in what we do. It is our existence as we walk the enlightened path leading us to blank. Our capacity and our will, will no longer be necessary as we change to our new existence.

ENLIGHTENMENT cont.

There is nothing that is happenstance. Everything is of purpose, although it may appear that way.

One couldn't help but be enlightened after experiencing things the way I did.

Like the mirror and the light, reflecting and emitting, I've come full circle in understanding my purpose.

I am a vehicle by which knowledge is to be disseminated.

The effervescence of life flowing through my veins reveals deeply, symbolism of which the mechanics I am still sorting out.

God is of Purpose that's why we must know that our makes exist.

Deleting these facts from our life do not make them out to be true.

The how and why will manifest in time. The everyday living is what we should be about.

There is no predetermined thought or afterthought or predestined knowledge that gets us any closer to the knowledge that God exists. What we have are testimonies and witnesses of the supernatural and divine. God and our makers give us signs. It has been this way since time immortal. What was left for us to discover, others will build upon and the riddle or puzzle will be that much more intriguing. Each new generation gets a combination. A key or code to the safe that needs to be cracked. We feel like we are busting open a hidden world and it has been put there for safe keeping.

But something will be revealed and we must pass through. A time warp of sorts acting as an exchange. The clearness separating our paths will reveal substance of another kind with images interspersed that are familiar.

We will be taken there, as we are following the light…perhaps at the never ending tunnel.

There is a world that opens up as a flight of passage. So I am not sure how significant the light is except for leading us there as we take our last breath and unbeknownst to us, are parting from our bodies.

The vehicle of transport was quite steady, landing in the clearness. I could hear its sound, humming in the background like a refrigerator, dead air from a TV, and the swishing noise it made when something opened up.

The entry to the portal was dim almost darkened to the point where you could only see huddles of (something) people talking in a group. I was in awe of its striking distance and revelation.

These were beings that I was familiar with otherwise why would I have felt so comfortable.

I was less frightened at the time and more in awe.

That the presence had revealed itself and I was not taken was phenomenal.

Especially after discussing the possibility of doing so.

Somehow I gather from that that it just wasn't my time. That I had been shown mercy or grace, and for whatever reason, given more time.

How could you not be an enlightened soul after such an experience? I was anointed. God had chosen me to give *an* answer.

****

Hindsight is 20/20 and clarity is simply a better explanation.

Clarity is the best understanding that we have when light is shown upon a situation. It is our perceptions that cloud our judgment.

Clarity and perception have nothing to do with right or wrong. It is the way we see it at the time.

Enlightenment is where the two twains meet.

That twilight of brightness in the sky riveting our soul as an awakening.

What is taught, can be gathered (clarity). What is felt, can be given (perceptions). But what is learnt, are lessons (enlightenment).

That which is relevant today may tomorrow become obsolete. We must seek to cherish ourselves and the blessings of life.

It is not up to me to sort out the madness of this world, only to not get caught up in it. That is the peace I must derive.

Being a victim of circumstance is not happenstance. It was meant to happen in the way in which it was.

Our truths are as beacons that stand out. And as they brightly shine, the probability of someone seeing them exactly the same is impossible. We may view things similar, and have similar beliefs, but our minds will process things different.

It is not likely that our souls will be enlightened at the same time.

Except, for when God comes for us. When all is shown that was hidden.

It is enlightenment that refreshes the soul and renders it anew. A new spirit awakening in the midst of a confusion.

I was jubilant when I lay there in the flesh - still alive! It wasn't that I was afraid of dying but truthfully speaking, leaving this world, was not an option. I still had things to do like so many others. That is why I understand that we will not be taken at the opportune time. I do not know what is in the other world. Familiar voices, people perhaps, but I do know that I wasn't ready to go there.

INTERLUDE

I am the burden bearer of my soul yet it is our thoughts that preclude us.

If we shed all that we've known than what's it all for? I have thoughts like this that dominate my mind. But the message I get is this:

We will shed all there is to bare of our burdens. We will shed our prior thoughts.

Maybe not in the physical sense that others can see us, but passing thorough as a bridge to get to the realm unknown. Surely it has always been there. Right beside us.

Enlightenment comes in the twilight. It is after our minds have rested. After racking our brains so much to get a clear answer. One that may or may not surprise us. It is the breakthrough that we live for. That and enjoying life to its fullest.

I live everyday knowing that something new will come.

No fears are present as I dream my life away. The dreams reflect my reality of days past and present. Filling gaps neatly tucked away for safe keeping. My storehouse of memories is impeccable at times but is also fuzzy and blurry. I have selective thoughts of things I want to do on this earth. There is nothing new under the sun, it is only expressed in a different way. Life is about making noise and letting someone know that you're there.

Our directors are our Angels and Guides leading us to knowledge that will enhance our purpose. The purpose of which is disseminated through time. Our Rings of Truth are our own, they are what we bear witness to. Rings of symbolism permeate our existence. We are married to them. Like bondage of slaves, these rings encase our natural spirit and render us hostage. These rings are: Perception, Clarity, Realism, Will and Power. All born of the natural spirit to embody them. They are emblems of who we are.

The rings of truth are the culmination of prior knowledge-past and present, disseminated through time.

The rings are of purpose thus leading to discovery.

Perception

You ask the question, what is the soul? What is its purpose? You could be dead on with your answer or dead wrong. Deception is the opposite of perception and in much fact based truth there could be lies. We must ask God for our directives as we seek clues.

God has already given us the gift of discernment therefore what we believe today can readily be discharged for new knowledge or better understanding.

Life's deception lurks in the shadows. It is reluctant to show up for fear of discovery. It can only be cast in the light. Even as it follows us it is the light that illuminates. Shadows display every move and as in the night, nothing is hidden. It is merely shaded.

That's why cameras are of no surprise. They capture the movement in the wake of the moment. We capture the shadows in the blink of an eye as it is being reflected.

Our lens provide depth of exposure and is constantly being sharpened with greater and keener focus.

Perceptions are born of our experience.

Our lens focus on that which we see but may not necessarily know. That which we don't see is speculative.

Walking in faith is our saving grace.

It is knowing that God(s) exist regardless of our doctrines, cultures or norms.

That god is greater than anything we could imagine or speculate on.

It may not always be what we believe or why or how we came to believe the way that we do, but that we 'Do Believe", is what's more important

God "is" and I "am." There are no bullet points that follow.

Self- fulfilling prophecy is understanding nature at its simplicity. There is no "matter" that cannot reveal itself except as God keeps it from being hidden.

Clarity

Clarity is the truth behind the curtain. Like sitting in a booth, it is the confessions that we make. Our mistakes become clearer once we've owned up to them and can see. The bottom line to anything is having full disclosure.

Realism is understanding that we are tied to this earth. That earth for now is our haven. As I walk this earth I think about the shadows. How, like the birds (crows) they seem to follow me. If I understood that my medium has a job to do, which is to warn me and protect me, then I must also understand that everything that exists of substance, is real. Realism is glazing at the stars and knowing that they are actually there even though high above. Or paddling in the stream where water is cradled by the earth. Matter is formed and regenerated. Its energy fields are massive and seem endless. We are bound here in space and time. Our substance touches everything that we feel. Our makeup is similar to others (the birds, the fish of the sea, the animals). We are travelers of the spirit waiting to take our place elsewhere. We know that everything has its place and time. Once we are buried we know that our life will be rejuvenated and new life will spring forth. A liquid substance feeds our matter supplying life sustaining qualities to every organ allowing them to function. That substance is pure in form and is called blood. Every creature has blood of some kind traveling through its veins. That is how we identify it as living. Mother- nature will take its course and the reality that we cannot escape this confinement will deftly set in. Everything is inter-connected and has its course in life. Realism is understanding that that is the way it is.

My **will** may determine my destiny or how far I will go. If my will is strong then so to am I. Frailties are not uncommon among us. We are limited by our bodies but strong as determined by our will. We are human and subject to any discomforts that humans may have, therefore our power is limited. Yet we are powerful beyond measure because power like beauty is in the eye of the beholder. My definition of power is the ability to control whether it be by brain or brawn.

Power has no face, culture or creed but power is an answer. Power is needed because we have the ability to be in control.

Therefore, if I am determined by my will to have power and seek clarity based on my perceptions, then whatever I do is done to suit my fancy. This is the way we live. Giving up power to someone else doesn't mean that we are powerless, it means that that is what we have chosen to do. We can always fight to regain that power back. Power over ourselves or others.

These rings are imminent. We adhere to them tightly. They tell our tale as we leave our markers in place.

.

.

3 RINGS OF TRUTH

RINGS OF TRUTH
In the
THOUGHTS OF A CLAIRVOYANT

I see through the lens of past and present

Dates and times aren't important

But people are.

And although I see the future that has come to present

I struggle with the now and what is.

Rectifying the Soul of a Clairvoyant

is impossible

For I will always be torn

between a twisted tale

and as Fate would have it- I see clear

clear enough to know that my

vision is warped

warped though time and space

as it passes through yet another.

****

The dreams are becoming more intense and also in succession.

The reality of interpretations has already become surreal. I would like for my dreams to not be true but have no control over them (the ones with dire consequences).

In my waking moments I cry. I become anxious with the thought of what just took place. If it is for me to be a medium and disseminate them-then what is the purpose?

I do not have the ability to intervene, only God does.

I have been shown a path that prayer stops things, halts them in motion-delaying them only until the inevitable time.

God hears us. God sees us. God knows us better than we know ourselves.

It is our faith that saves us. Our belief in the almighty force that is reckoning us to that day. Readying and preparing us for our entry into another place.

Our departure is inevitable. Our faith and belief in it is not.

We believe that we will live and die then maybe not live again. But there are two signs that tell us otherwise.

It is not for us to know the answers. There is no living breathing human being that's been here before and come back to tell us about it.

We have been brought to the brink of illusion. Some of us, many of us, have seen the light.

We have seen similitudes of our way forward. But disseminating that too others that haven't seen it is complicated.

It's complicated because the world is made up for the living it is not made for the dead.

The dead must move on when they pass away.

They have been shown a gift. The gift of life.

But death is not a curse nor the punishment. Death is a passage in time.

For those that believe in the hereafter, hold on to that faith.

There is something to come. Something that's present, even now, right before us.

But we can't touch or feel it because it exists through and around us. Surrounding our body with effervescence of life. It is the clearness that separates the divide.

We live, we eat, drink, speak and function through what the clearness embodies every day. It is our life force that separates us from death.

It causes us to see, to move, to live. When our body cavity gives out on us-the Clearness that we share will continue to be there.

We must embrace that which surrounds us like a hug and a kiss-we are bound to it.

Recognizing that the clearness has attributes that are life sustaining and forces we can use to our advantage. God gives us qualities that complement one another. Naked in our souls we bury the hidden truths. The balance of life is contained within us.

We must succumb to the dark just as much as we must take a breath. Our body rests before its active state. Regardless of what we're doing the clearness remains.

Under the cloak of night or twilight as the moon and stars shine, it is clear on purpose and with the purpose of showing us the way.

The allegory of living in sin is a misnomer. It is not the sin that we do but the lack of faith. We will pay for our deeds as they come full circle-that's the order of things in life. Evil and horrendous acts perpetrated on others will find its way back to you. That is the sin as we know it. It cannot be written in a tablet or a paper bound in a book. It is scribed within our hearts when our brains are functioning right. The difference between right and wrong is within your measure of faith. God sees all. Once we acknowledge that, our deeds become acts leaning towards that which is good.

We must battle the innate forces we are bequeathed with. We came here given a fighting chance to win our battles. God gives everyone a chance to live. The life cycle must take its course. If it seems shortchanged it is because every act must be carried out. Only the force of God can stop it.

We grow and become old, we wither and die. We cannot garner all there is to know, there is no purpose. We must share in the dreams and accolades of others. We must bear witness to testimonies of truth as they are bestowed upon us. Contrived faith is not an answer. Our prescripts for life are compactly sealed. We are living legends in our own time. We are cohorts in a movement of time expressing our passions to the height of our abilities. We don't know what the future holds but the future embraces our forethought, precluding our destiny and delineating markers along the way. We live as vessels of one another learning to love. If we love our brethren, then we can love ourselves. The mirror will spawn new truths every time you look in it. Our actions dictate who we are and our familial bonds tie us.

My inspiration remains my constants- my mother as she wept, my father as a hero, my sons and daughters whom I have still yet to claim. My siblings that taught me so well, that life is a shared moment. My parents as my caretakers and guardians served as my guides answering gods call to do their duty.

Their truths may or may not have become mine but their labor of love was significant. As I instill into my young their brief hearts of sacrifice they too, must understand that the life and death process is a continuum that must sustain itself. Life needs death to remain and death needs life to continue on. We feed and nourish ourselves from this enriching environment. Earth replenishes constantly. The duality of forces is contained within the clearness. God is in control at all times.

It is not up to us to decide our fate. We can merely define what should be in it. Our paths are clear and chosen. The roots we dig up, the roads we follow and conditions that are present all are indicative of a pre-destiny. We will play out our parts as if acting on a stage. Our expiration stamps serve as inspiration. We know that time will not standstill only moments of clarification and glory as we define it when we stop to revel in justification. It is expedient that we live as though we will remain.

We take nothing and lavish in thought. Our containment is meant for confinement. Protection from perhaps other worlds.

Our mediums of exchange operate on levels unknown. Nothing tangible greets the eye except beauty and wasteland. We know that it is difficult to achieve our highest hopes because they have become distant from our reach. Reaching up to congregate with God, to communicate is the ultimate decision one can make. But it is the Clearness that sends wavelengths. Our thoughts are unseen and must travel. Traveling to a distance and speed of resounding cheer. Our negligent past will catch up to our productive future all we have to do is put our hands on it and touch it and it is real. Then the reality of the Clearness and the blank wall traveling like the clouds blocking us from seeing anything other than what is right before us. The clouds move with a whisk to seal what's above. A blank wall is our life unwritten, unscripted and to no avail can we take any of our markers with us nor our faith. Our prescripts will shed with each step we take towards the light. Any and all subscriptions (doctrines) will be left behind as God shows us the path forward. It is to our destiny that we have arrived.

I do not know what is in the other side but I do know that God(s) has been reaching down conversing with me. It is the ultimate healing to be seen with and walk with our makers and God.

****

An Ending must be as Powerful as its Beginning

When someone comes back, it is usually for the other person. This is what I have found out.

Rya was my daughter's very good friend. They were inseparable and she was like a second mother to her.

She must have known that my daughter had been worried about her as she didn't get to say her goodbyes. Everything happened so quickly and so suddenly that she was gone before we knew it. I think she wanted me to know as well. This child in the dream was happy with faceless expressions. She wanted her to know that she was ok. That's what I told her. I spared many of the details telling her only the pleasant parts. But I did not spare anything when relaying it to my younger daughter. The one I had tried to wake the night I had it.

"Umm, she said. Well, we don't know what that means, and hopefully nothing's going to happen."

I held on to what she said, grasping for straws and with some ray of hope. She said, I shouldn't worry. But I knew otherwise.

I half- heartedly shared my dream with my oldest daughter, the one it was intended for, telling her only the good parts. Normally that's not something I'd do, tell only half a dream. But the message I felt was meant for her. I was the medium by which to let her know. I hadn't made full sense of it yet and could only tell her what I garnered. It was Rya coming back to tell me she was OK and I was to pass that on. The person in the dream never showed her entire face but had the mannerisms and gestures of someone just like her and dressed the way she did. She wore a soft wool camel jacket and brown polyester pants. She appeared to be happy and free, dancing in the wind as if she had no care in the world.

The water was beautiful and clear, like the sky above it. Its deepness reflected the row of shimmering boats stacked so neatly across. There was a mirror image of the peaceful terrain that looked pleasant to the eye. I reveled momentarily in delight while in the dark recesses still disturbed.

Soft waves hit the shore line like petals brushing up against the rocks. Swarms of ducks rode the pool tides while keeping their distance. My walk would turn into a fast jog eventually if I was to keep pace with my exercise. I had built up to a sweat now with my workout, but it had taken awhile. I'd come here every day for the same purpose- losing weight and staying in shape. But my ritual had turned into so much more. This had now become my peaceful spot. My place of serenity in the early morning. Rain, sleet or frost I would be there. But this day was one of the loveliest of its kind.

In the dream I had saw her stopping, taking the time to swing her braids. She twirled her head round and round with big gestures and swayed them back and forth. It was like a child amiss of anything. Oblivious to anything remotely connected to responsibility. Free as a bird she acted as if the wind would set her free. She danced, she played, she giggled, and she laughed. Playing as a child with no cares or worries. Her breath was in sync and tune with the birds. I got it, I thought about it further. God had released her in the wind with the likeness and spirit of a child running hapless and free. I knew it was her from the clothes she was wearing. Either her or could've been my daughter. My daughter was a mini version of her. They even dressed the same.

There was a dual message I was receiving. One was pretty clear, the other one fuzzy. I didn't know what quite to make of it.

Cross my heart and hope to die, I'd say this as a little girl whenever I made a promise about something. Taking it all in, I'd promised myself that I'd never let this message die. It was to be shared with the world along with my daughter.

I could not make a mockery of its meaning although I was upset at first to its purpose. I had questioned why she had taken so long (in the dream) to come help the ailing person, the person who it appeared was dying yet still alive. Whose body had dwindled yet was crying out for help. I was glad this dream turned into something pure and good that something meaningful could be gotten out of it. But I also knew that something else was brewing. Something that would go right along with this happy time.

I stepped out of the park (that day) saying that everything was going be alright. Jubilant to tell my children that the story (well dream) would end up bright.

Inspired by the chain of events, I wrote a poem that day on Facebook, and it went like this:

Written Nov 29 2012 on fb

"The sunlight beamed down like petals on my face. The raindrops raced to bring me a kiss. The morning dew woke me like a fresh spring shower. A light passed by and cast me its flickering beam. Fragrant flowers lined the shore. The magic of the ocean swished its sounds much like the humming birds above singing in the trees. I began to dance, giggle and twirl. Thinking happy thoughts and releasing them to the wind. #signed: a child of God#"

****

But it was the second dream that got me. The one that came the next few days in succession.

I sat up in the middle of the night after the second dream (Dream # 9) and shouted, NOOOOOO!!! I said as loud as I could with the sounds reverberating off the walls. The outburst could have woken the neighbors. I held it for as long as I could without regard for who heard me. This was the first time I'd questioned God for fear that this reality would happen. I jumped at the thought of it. I rocked back and forth in full panic mode wishing that the dream would go away. I didn't ever want to sleep again for fear that it would come true. I held onto the covers tightly clenching them with my teeth to keep me quiet. My arms wrapped around my body tightly embracing myself since no one else could. I was scared. Truly shaken at the thought of this dream coming true. I don't think that that had ever happened before, not the way it did this time. I was captured in the moment of truth, of awakening. I braced my back against the headboard thrusting myself upright. I tucked pillows behind my back to make sure I wouldn't want to lay on them. The headboard braced me up so that I couldn't fall asleep again. I didn't want the possibility of continuing my dream. That particular dream was gut, wrenching, as if it were snatching something from my soul. I cried. The night was long.

My phone call to my daughter was right away. I held the receiver in my hand. It went straight to voicemail. Hum, how expedient I thought. If she couldn't help me, who could.

I needed to stay awake.

It would be a marathon-of sleep deprivation.

It was me who called out to God alone and desperate. That God could hear me would be all I needed.

No God, let this not be true!

Something shook me as never before as if I knew something would manifest.

If fell back to sleep eventually but it wasn't before morning and it wasn't before talking to my youngest daughter.

"I will never go back to sleep again, I yelled.

Why, what happened?

I told her the dream.

She was more silent than complacent. She didn't coddle me as she did before when I told her the last one. I could sense hesitation in her voice and concern.

You know, I have been seeing a lot of crows, she said.

As disturbing as it was, here is that dream:

Dream #9

The railroad tracks were hard to cross. They seemed harder with two kids in tow. Where I was going I didn't know. It was to a building that was on the other side of the tracks and that seemed far away. I was reluctant to go there with the burden of taking the kids but at the same time anxious. My sister had called me (in my dream) to tell me I needed to be with family and that I was the only one missing. I told her it would be impossible if I had to bring the children. I somehow showed up at a white building that was the destination. My cousin expressed his disappointment with me when I arrived by showing a stern yet frowning face. He was angry that I had took so long to get there. I entered the building which was like a concert hall. I sat down but felt compelled to walk down to the center stage. When I reached it I felt as if I was in the presence of someone familiar. Someone I loved. This turned out not to be a concert after all and the person was my mother. (Later on, after the dream -the exact events played out).

"This can't be true!" I voiced inside in the middle of the night. As if the first dream I'd had a few days before wasn't enough. I didn't dare lay my head back down as tired as I was although the pillow was inviting. I wobbled back and forth nodding my head in the process trying to stay awake. If I went back to sleep that meant continuing my dream or possibly actually seeing the outcome. I was devastated and did not want to go back to sleep ever again. I knew that if the dream manifest it would be devastating. I pressed and held my head tight against the backboard supporting and sat erect. I couldn't go back to sleep or lay down again. Not ever. Going back to sleep meant that the dream might continue. I wished it away. But it was too late.

My daughter was astonished at my decision upon hearing it later that morning. I had told her the dream.

Umm, she said. Well, we don't know what that means, and hopefully nothing's going to happen.

I held on to what she said, grasping for straws and with some ray of hope. She said, I shouldn't worry. But I knew otherwise.

My mom come to get her. That's why it was her in the dream. She came and got her daughter and eased her transition. And Rya came to tell me my daughter would be ok-happy and free with no worries. This was the message I was to ultimately receive.

No worries, no pain, because there should be none.

I wanted many times to transfer my daughter's pain onto myself. I would have easily stood in her shoes to take her place. But there was no need. She was stronger than I in the situation. Many times I wanted to break down and cry at the thought of what could be or what this may or may not be doing to her. But instead I held it in. just as I did my sister. When I held her hand at the hospital in her final days, it was in light of the dream, of not knowing. I had put the dream in the back of my mind worried only about her immediate circumstances until it kept being thrust before me. The images of my mother laying there in a casket and in an awkward position I couldn't describe. But it was not her, my mother had long since passed away and I knew it. It was her warm embrace of one of her daughters that she had so loved. I understood. My first born was going through her most trying time as well. I found myself standing in my mother's shoes trying to fulfill them with love dignity and grace.

I cried for my mother. I cried for my sibling. I cried for my daughter. One much older and had battled her ailment for quite some time and one much younger and newly diagnosed. Both were strong and capable of beating the odds and oddly enough my sibling had already won her battle for many years. If I could ever be so blessed to have my daughter do the same if not eradicated completely and cured. But God had a hand in this and I knew it. I knew about the succession of dreams that had appeared before. The many recent deaths I had come to know and taken so hard. This too shall pass I surmised and hopefully in the best light.

I had interacted with both my sibling and cousin in the dream and they were the most significant counterparts while I was away on my visit. I also had noticed in retrospect that I had took the train. The very same train that was holding me up in my dream. It was too long, I worried and had stood in the way. It was prolonging me from reaching my destination. I had tried so hard to get where I was going (in the dream) to see the person I loved but didn't know who it was and that needed me. I was to see them one last time and pay my respects. I knew it was someone close because family was present. My sister told me I needed to hurry up and be with the family. Ironically this is exactly what I was rushing to do on the train. The airplane flights were too costly for last minute travel although I would have readily paid had I known it was much more- dire at the time. I had arrived in time and on time for my engagement. The engagement God had sent me on only I didn't know it. It was the last time I'd see my loved one. Moments together with her were precious. I counted down the minutes and the hour that I knew she could be strong. Her kids were resilient. They showed the side of her that she had taught them well. Loving and kindness poured from their hearts to everyone-it couldn't have been any other way because she was kind herself. Always giving her last and sharing she had an open door policy for anyone that needed help. I called my siblings domain the refugee house. She cared about everybody and was very close to her own; her kids, her family. She was one of the greatest persons I knew and the best big sister one could possibly have. It had nothing to do with what she accomplished in life. In fact, nothing I'm speaking of is tangible. It was the innate ability she had to love unconditionally and be loved by many as she opened her arms and embraced folks. She didn't care if you were rich or poor, in her eyes you were all the same.

That is a quality I learned from her-to judge by character not by the depths of constraints. If you needed her, she was there. She tried her best to give of herself wholeheartedly even when faced when obstacles and struggles, I too admired this. In some respects, she was a mini me of my mom and her only daughter a reflection and mini me of her. The cycle would continue although my niece I encouraged her to walk in her own shoes. People had expectations. Her mother's shoes would be too big to fill because before she had her she had already laid the foundation. I am proud of her children the young men and women they have become. She set the example like my mother to be strong, put family first and to open your heart to others as others would need it even when they didn't think they needed it themselves. Selfless love is the way to describe it. No wonder my mother's loving arms embraced her and eased her transition. If heaven is where they'll reside, I wouldn't be surprised.

I took the trip not knowing what to expect. Her sick I guess, but with a full recovery. Never once did I go up there thinking that the dream would play out. In fact, I was suppressing it the whole time until visuals of what I saw in my dream kept coming to the forefront and interacting as to no longer conceal what the dream meant.

Still I left hopeful just as I was when I traveled there. But on the trip back I had some alone time, without the lady sitting next to me and gabbing away about things I knew nothing of and was oblivious too. She wanted to make the whole trip a historic scenic reference to whatever it is she thought important. Although I liked her and thought she was nice and kind she was really rather annoying. I just wanted to sleep on the way there. The exhaustion of dealing with the realities of my own daughter and what she faced were bearing down on me. And now to face my sister in her time of need as well, it was unfathomable.

I relished in the quiet moments only to think that everything would be good if I thought happy thoughts. I fell asleep soundly, only to be awaken by a ring from my phone. I was in route back home but after speaking with my sister knew I might need to return, but between traveling there and getting home there were mixed messages because my sister had pulled through before and this time my prayer was that she would again.

I sat home after a few days not entirely pleasant with worries beginning to surmount. I would need to make every chemo appointment with my daughter. That was the least I could do as her mother. And since I couldn't take it away, I would lay there right next to her as if it were me that were taking her pain away and with each infusion I felt that way. She on the other hand, read her scriptures, sat them on the table next to her when she wasn't reading them and held them in the forefront as if they were her guiding force. I loved that fact that she loved God and God was taking care of her regardless of what the future possessed. I knew that she was armored with faith as her shield and belief in the almighty (regardless of what religion she was affiliated with) and that that would see her through no matter what the outcome. I believed as she believed that having faith was the answer.

It wasn't long before my biggest fear had come into play. Everything in the dream had played out. I belted in pain, that whopping cry that hurt so deep even your belly can't hold it in. My inward screams could no longer be held. Someone dear to me had decided to exit gracefully as she knew it was her time to go. If I could ever be so strong as to have at least an ounce of her courage, or strength, maybe I could be half the woman that she was.

I loved her then, I love her now and always.

My cousin that was in my dream held my hand. He was standing right beside me and I didn't know it. He was upset with me in the dream and stood erect and tall wearing a nice suit as if he was guarding something. In the dream he was mad at me because I had chosen to leave when he thought I should be inside like the rest of my family. In the dream he snubbed me and wouldn't speak to me. But in reality he embraced me as we cried together holding me against his shoulder.

I thought about it later on and asked, "why him?" Of all my kinfolk that I love so much and could have interacted with, why the one that came to me in my dream? It was meant to be I told myself. It was a reminder of the characters who were the ones most important in getting me the messages of my dream that things were urgent, I needed to be there, and this was an important event that I shouldn't take lightly as if it wouldn't happen.

That is what I garnered from it in retrospect. That god had braced me for the inevitable just as it has happened many times before. The Chain of events, the chains of my lineage, the chain to remain unbroken until once again when it was time.

I yelled so hard for my dearly departed loved one that I don't remember the last time I cried like that except when I stood up against my bedpost denying any part of it in the dream.

It hurt so bad I could have fainted. I held inside much more than anyone knew about my sister and my daughter. That events had already played out beforehand.

I was tested with my faith at that moment. That God was disseminating this information to me in an uncanny way seemed to me to be a breach of my trust. Why did I have to receive it in riddles, puzzles, and dreams? All I knew is that it had all happened, that I had seen it before, and there was nothing, absolutely nothing that I could have done about it.

I call this an un-daunting faith. When you have been touched by the hands of God in all your queries and still remain sane in your darkest moments, deepest secrets, and darkest hours.

Although you have to sometimes question it, if the "kook" is really you, like the nurse from the hospital had said.

Was she giving a message of some sort, ahead of time perhaps? "They cannot help you, she said no one can". I will remember that phrase the rest of my life. The infamous doctor she was referring too was clueless as to her whereabouts or comments. I'm the only one that heard it. Thus I have to conclude that the message was meant for me. I would be the one misunderstood-if and whenever I would talk about it.

These were my interactions with the mediums that God chose to send to me on our Makers behalf as an intercessor of some sort. I was to see the beyond and what was in it. The entities, the beings, the characters that played out in the bodies of folks who were unaware. I have to conclude that that is what it's about. Much more than I can fathom when my weary brain queries and more grandeur than most or any of us can ever expect. Once again I have been touched by the almighty power that is present in all our situations. Once again I was given a glimpse of what was to come. A clairvoyance if you will. A vision of some sort. That is why after my loved one departed I couldn't type a word for weeks or months. Even though these thoughts were fresh in my brain. And for a period of time after my daughter's chemo and radiation treatments were finished, I didn't want to think about, know, or process anything. But from time to time I would revisit the accounts of what took place attempting very feebly to put it in perspective. With the exception of my daughter I wanted the outcome of my dreams to be so very different.

I wanted my loved one to still be here and have more time. That's why I realized that was my mother's way of coming back. To help ease my pain. I had questioned before (in my first book) why others had chosen to come back and deliver a message but she hadn't. I assumed it was because I was the closest to her having been her daughter but my father did and I was just as close to him. But he wasn't my confident. My mother had been. I had told her everything about the dreams I was having and still had while she was alive. As my parent, she knew the inner depths of my soul better than I knew myself. How could she not come for her child? I want to say thank you mother for helping me to understand how deep your love is for us, your children. It is my personal testament as to knowing that it would you to set us free. Free as birds flying in the wind on angelic and magical wings. You set us free in life and once again will have the task of setting us free in death. Our exit must be as powerful and grand as our entry, mother dearest. I understand now-and I thank you for that.

Two lives fulfilled that's what I call it. The one where I have to rectify the soul with its calling and purpose and the one where I have to walk amongst (everyday) folk knowing that I've already channeled my inner child and been touched. The Gift I carry in my soul is far more powerful than the strides I take in life. The gift that must somehow be passed on and shared with others who will relive it and either lift or increase my burden. I have prayed to God many times for the relief and was therefore told to just live. To live life merry and be happy, as normal life is intended.

So at this moment, I feel released.

I'll admit one minor fault: that I still close closet doors as I walk by them. This is out of fear of striking up another conversation with the Ogre. This is not a fear of death, dying, or the unknown. But fear that's engrained so deeply showing what the Almighty is capable of it becomes a Reverence out of awe and respect. Some boundaries I feel I shouldn't cross or at bare the soul to strike up a conversation. I think somehow that I will meet the Ogre again, one day. It is the angel of death stalking and inevitable that our paths will meet. But in the meantime I am not hastening any encounters. Being blessed, is the best descriptor I have for it.

When two halves make a whole, our destiny is fulfilled. We were put here to promulgate the species and keep it going. Everything else is consequential, our politics, the rituals we muster up, our belief systems written in stone. Everything is breakable and thus earth shakable. Nothing is permanent and fixed except time and space. In fact it is space through which we travel. The timing of that travel is irrelevant to man only to God and our Makers. We have no clue as to when it will be our time to go. We cannot hasten or delay it. That travel plan has already set and can be intervened at any time. We are not the interveners, the saviors or savers of our own lives. We are the energy which travels forward as we shed our bodies when we leave this earth. Many philosophers have discovered this. I call it the bridge to the divide. It is the Happening that is inevitable for all of us. To be "Taken" (alive) in another form of existence. There is no unspoken truth to this. It is at the very core of our belief system and the one fiber that holds the common thread. Most people believe that God is in command and can intervene at any time and that it is a misnomer to forget that. For how could we be more powerful than that which put us here? Our stop gaps don't allow us to see the divide but it was here all along. Our brain is prepared to function letting us see the light as a whole once we step into it. But it is God that shields us from it and thus relates it in increments to prepare us for our fate. We have a meeting with our maker and it is destined and bound to happen. The preparations we make for ourselves will be of naught other than knowing that it will happen. We can never shield ourselves from that which is non-shielding. We are as gullible as a newborn babe lying in the street. The only way of the cars to avoid hitting it is by divine intervention. But all acts must play out regardless of their consequence.

I have to think that maybe just maybe I can view death as a passageway and somehow that will make it more palatable. But I think not. I too have fears like everyone else as to what, where and when that fate will catch up with me. It is not the death (the act) that I fear because I have come close to and seen the moment. The fear is of the natural order of things and where I will find my place. I do believe since it is not of my choosing (to die) then when it happens I likely won't remember it anyway and that is my solace.

Blank is the state we will leave in shedding all wants and desires. A comprehensive plan is where we will be going taking our place among others to do what perhaps we may have always done, time-warp our way into new adventures. Or maybe we will be the overseers of our loved ones that will reside after we remain in another state as our markers have chosen for us. Frozen in time like the ice with impressions as memories.

Yell. Scream. Stomp. Cry all you want. Shout out hallelujah and praise God.

Our markers are fixed and permanent as long as the ice keeps them. Our deeds are everlasting and imprinted upon societies membrane and perhaps even written down as eternal scrolls of pages to be turned.

Whatever we've done (while we're here) God has no need for it where we are going.

That's why Blank is the state in which we will find ourselves leaving in although all the while resisting as if our words, actions and deeds really mean something. We want credit for what we've done, perhaps something good. We want credit for the way we think, walk and dress. But what we failed to realize is that it was all on borrowed time. Our time was fixed when we got here. We used what God had provided to enhance our living. What was at stake the whole time was our souls not our bodies. Our bodies were vulnerable and fragile like our minds. The mechanism in which Our Makers chose to put us in was shielded. It had already built in protectors. We had ribs as our armor to protect as a vest and vital organs. We had a skull as a helmet to house and protect the very thing we hold in high esteem (our brain). And our body cavity is in synch with the oceans and waves from which it drinks and feeds. We were put here as part of the continuum, the rest we don't know.

But what I was shown lets me know with certainty that there is so much more!

I live among the Saints knowing that I have been touched. They too were just ordinary people with extraordinary experiences. Experiences only God could have allowed. We will all have them, in our own time.

We don't know which medium God has chosen to act on your behalf. It has to be of reference, something that's familiar and you already know. But it will be given as patterns and riddles for us to guess and decide what that message is conveying. Gods promise is not how you will know but that you will know. And it is like the earth and all its blessings-to be discovered. In the meantime, just know that we grow and mature and have obstacles to overcome similar to every other creature that exists. I can't communicate with those animals for them to tell us what that is. All we know is that we coexist right along beside them and share the resources of this earth. The containment is shared with many others some of like kind some not. Their destiny is just as profound as ours I can guarantee it. Don't underestimate the power of a being that God has created. What we think may beneath us today may have dominion over us tomorrow, who's to say? But what we do know about the many creatures that exist, we don't know all of them and they don't all of us. Their worlds are separate as the division has already taken place. Like kind must be with like kind and that is a metaphor it has nothing to do with like species. Like species come in all shades shapes and forms but none is superior over the other. It is our antics that dictate what shape and form we choose to be in because we can readily mix amongst ourselves therefor similarities do exist amongst our many cultures.

Life is a continuum not a bargaining chip for heralding faith. We complete ourselves when the cycle completes and that I'm afraid will take care of itself all on its own.

AFTER THE CHEMO

Days spent with my daughter have been happy and carefree. I don't know if this was by design or mother-nature taking its course. I do know that she was the one that planned the events. A nice romp on the beach in the late afternoon melding into the evening just in time to catch the sunset glimmering upon the water.

The nice stroll in the park where the kids ran ahead of us tracing the landscapes and fields. And the pleasant afternoon where the swimming pool seemed to be waiting for us.

Time was not at a standstill but kept whisking away as if it was. The clock didn't need to be watched when we were having so much fun.

Her attitude and charm went right along with it-as if nothing, nothing could stand in her way.

There was a tranquil calm and peace about her that I couldn't put my fingers on.

For someone who had just been in the trenches battling cancer like she was, other than the few times that she would take off her hat, you wouldn't even know it. And even then with her nicely shaped and clean shaven head you would think she could pose for the cover of a magazine.

No jokes or slurs could be thrown her way because she was beautiful. But it was her beauty inside that was resonating on these days.

I could see in her eyes the deep convictions of love and family commitment.

Her bible studies had done wonders as far as her faith. She could walk with the angle of a queen holding her head up high-although I knew that her body had been on the battlefield but would not be torn apart.

The cancer hadn't spread and was caught in time to shrink it.

Now we were waiting for the miracle of it being zapped away.

We both knew only God could work wonders like that. Both she and I knew in our hearts and any unspoken words between us were heartfelt. The nature of our exchange was flowing free. I could tell sometimes when I looked in her eyes that she wanted answers-a better explanation perhaps, than the ones she had been given.

But her bible was her armor and she wore it like a glove close to her breast and bosom where the ailment lay underneath. It was as if by doing this she could cling to the book she felt that she so desperately needed.

I loved to see my child acting this way. Loving God as I myself love her, unconditional and without remorse.

If the spirit of the words could only remove that which was making her sick. Her vowels were readily apparent. She was a Christian by faith, believer at heart and a child of God.

No one could move her or shake her faith-not even the possibility of facing death if she didn't rid herself of this deadly disease.

I thanked God for my angel. For allowing me to grace the stage with her as we walk this earth. Her fortitude showed me that mine was nothing compared to hers. For I wouldn't know what I'd do faced with the same set of circumstances.

Being one step removed was no condolence. I walked with her and held her hand. I made it a point to sit through all the chemo sessions.

It wasn't as if I wanted to feel them but perhaps take her pain away and transpose it into my body. Lying beside her the moment the medicine was going in was my way of letting her know she was not alone. And although she was embraced by the embodiment of her Maker, that she could also be rocked in the bosom of her mother.

I needed her as much as she needed me.

If we have chosen our subscriptions in life, then we must have faith. Our doctrines are our prescriptions fulfilled but it is God that will do the ultimate healing.

The light is a beacon of kindness passing shadows our way and letting us wonder in its gaze. Our spirits leave our bodies traveling at speeds greater than we can. The protective shield that once housed us are now ready to release. They served their purpose and shall now be returned to that from which they came-the earth. Shedding our past to be propelled into our future is an ominous duty that must be performed. It is a rite of passage to the stars and beyond. Our souls held the answers all the time to our living. We were encased as our mediators guided and led us. In times of sorrow, someone was there. In times of grief as well as gratitude we were afforded a way. The accidents we were prone to were often times near misses as whispers were planted in our brain to react just in the nick of time. Fight or flight they called it. But I knew, that our watchers, our makers, and our guides intervened. We had helpers. We always did. We always do. And when that time comes to meet them, we will.

It doesn't matter the name you call upon in time of distress, help or need. What Ever makes you comfortable or suits your fancy is what God ALLOWS.

THIS WAY NO ONE IS EXCLUDED FROM HEAVEN OR EARTH AS IT IS WRITTEN.

>   There are always chances to re-enter or exit.

BOWELS OF THE SHIP

The next dream wasn't my last but it played a significant part in solidifying everything that I had known. That I was the one to tell the story of how life entered and exited our clan. I could see with clarity the purposeful ways in which stories unfolded with departure as its destiny. Reentering was speculative at best but a real answer to this mystical quandary.

Sometimes answers are "slipped in" in a purposeful way to make my mind gravitate towards its meaning. The ticker tape scenario was a good justification of that. Once again I was implanted with thought almost impregnated with wisdom beyond measure. I couldn't fathom what it all must have been for but I could tell that I had left the room enlightened.

We must be born again and fulfill the promise. We are recycled, renewed, rejuvenated at random times unbeknownst to us. We are readied for the process before we are reentered.

This dream will have its lasting effects because of all the dreams I had this one actually placed me there. I had entered the bowels of the ships. It was a portal providing an entryway for transport. I don't know if the ship was parked but it gave off this humming sound. I can almost compare it to the sound I'd heard before when it appeared in my living room. This time I was standing there in what the woman called. "The Bowels of the Ship." God had once again given me a glimpse of what takes place in our passage. We are processed.

I landed in a bright room surrounded by trash. There was debris strewn everywhere as if I had needed to clean it up. I stepped over it around it and moved forward. Then I passed through an open door into another room. This room was dimly lit with impeccably laid carpet all around. It was held up by beams distanced from each other. There was recessed lighting posts on the walls that added to its decorative trim. I could see that the room was well kept and somewhat inviting. In the rear of the room was a figure. It was approaching taking regular steps. The figure was tall and partially hidden by the dampened light. The figure kept walking and was impeccably dressed. Her clothes were well tailored, like a cashmere sweater and wool pants. As she came closer I could see that her hair was cut short in a bob that cropped her face. She appeared to be tanned, maybe a caramel or light color. With the darkened light I couldn't tell. No facial features were shown, once again, as with the shadows before, her face was hidden. She walked with determination headed n my direction. I stood enamored not saying a word. When she was up close she reached past me and grabbed a hand. It was the hand of the floating lady that was appearing beside me. She had come from the rear out of nowhere. She was standing erect moving forward, wearing a white gown and her arms straight down her sides.

She appeared to not be aware of her surroundings or what was happening to her. She kept floating until they met each other on my right side. the tall lady reached out to grab her hand and turned in the opposite direction to lead her back down the aisle and corridor with her. Where they were going I had no clue. I could see them walking off in the distance with their backs turned but right before she left she turned her head over her shoulder so I could see. She flashed her face in order to let me see before she departed. My mouth dropped open as I could see that the face unlike the body, did not appear human. The darkness was present and the light gleamed only a little to show its contents. There was enough for it to forever remain a mystery.

Elongated body, towering towards the sky, where had I seen that before? This time it was walking in my presence. The figure also had been perturbed with me. It didn't want me there and made gestures as it approached and passed. I felt as if I was intruding on sacred territory while witnessing an event. An event of passage that was taking place while someone was being readied for the process. The person floating felt very familiar. The tall lady handled her gently as if she was special. Someone had placed me there to observe. I had awakened from my dream by now and knew it was real.

.

EPILOGUE

My familial ties have a lot to do with my being selected. I felt in many ways that possibly stemming from way back in my lineage there was a deep connection. If I could look at my history tree to examine any of my ancestors to determine which were given instructions to pass on the knowledge that our forbearers wanted us to exchange, I could get better vision of why it was now my turn. I think that in each lineage there is made the sacrifice of a soul bearer who takes on the culmination of collective lives among the clan and who will have a direct link to that which is broken or not sustained. Sickness, illness, health and wealth are all among the visions though it is clear that mine are limited in scope when it comes to spatial or tactical ramifications. There is no way that I can pin down an event in order to supersede, circumvent, or alter altogether any wave length that the event is traveling on. It is likely that it must travel through time and space on a collision course to make its fate with destiny. I have a duty to report all events in real time. This way I know that I am the official time recorder of any extraordinary event. I am sometimes compelled to have this special gift passed along in the twilight to someone else. Maybe in the next generation.

It is with love and special meaning that I write this book.

ABOUT THE AUTHOR

Ihsan Jones resides in Northern California where she works in corporations and in starting new business ventures. She holds a Master of Science in Cybersecurity. As an entrepreneur, her passion has been to share her experiences to benefit others.

www.ingramcontent.com/pod-product-compliance
Lightning Source LLC
LaVergne TN
LVHW041633070426
835507LV00008B/598